CLOUDED SKY

Clouded Sky

Miklós Radnóti

REVISED EDITION

TRANSLATED FROM THE HUNGARIAN BY

STEVEN POLGAR

STEPHEN BERG

S. J. MARKS

THE SHEEP MEADOW PRESS
Riverdale-on-Hudson, New York

Some of the poems in this volume appeared as follows:

"Love Poem," "Night," "The Red Flower," "Picnic in May," "In Hiding," and the "Postcards: 2, 3, 4" in *Colorado State Review*, Vol. II, No. 3, Summer, 1967. Copyright © 1967 by *Colorado State Review*, (which is now published under the title *TransPacific*).

"Night," "In Hiding," and the "Postcards: 2, 3, 4" in *The Nation*, Vol. 205, No. 14, October 30, 1967.

"Spain, Spain," "Love Poem," "Clouded Sky," "The Red Flower," and "Picnic in May" in *Delos*, No. 1, 1968.

"Goats," "Friday," and "Two Fragments" in *Stony Brook*, Nos. 1/2, Fall, 68.

"December," "In Your Arms," "Charm," and "I Hid You" in *December*, Vol. X, No. 1, Fall, 1968.

Postcards (1,2,3,4), published as a pamphlet by The Cummington Press, 1969.

"Hesitating Ode," "Friday," "If You Listen to Me...," "With Your Right Hand on the Back of My Head," and the "Postcards: 1, 2, 3, 4" in *Modern Poetry in Translation*, 6, 1970.

"Red Shore" and "Roots" in *Stand*, Vol. II, No. 4, 1970.

"Charm," "Maybe...," "Two Fragments," and "Song" in *The London Magazine*, 1972.

Clouded Sky was reprinted in its entirety in *Poetry East*, No. 22, 1987.

Printed on acid-free paper in the United States. This book meets the guidelines for permanence and durability of the Committee on Production Guidelines for Book Longevity of the Council on Library Resources.

Library of Congress Cataloging-in-Publication Data

Radnóti, Miklós, 1909-1944.
 [Tajtékos ég. English]
 Clouded sky / Miklos Radnoti ; translated from the Hungarian by Steven Polgar, Stephen Berg, S. J. Marks.-- Rev. ed.
   p. cm.
 ISBN 1-931357-12-9 (alk. paper)
 I. Polgar, Steven, 1946- II. Berg, Stephen. III. Marks, S. J. IV.
 Title.
 PH3321.R27T313 2003
 894'.511132--dc21

2003008562

We are grateful to the New York State Council on the Arts, a state agency, for their support.

Contents

Spain, Spain   1

Federico García Lorca   2

Autumn and Death   3

At an Impatient Hour   5

Thursday   6

For an Edition of *The Steep Road*   7

Early Summer   8

Song   10

Love Poem   11

Two Fragments   12

Fires   13

Simple-Minded Song About My Wife   14

Like Death   15

Clouded Sky   16

Maybe . . .   18

In My Memories   20

Red Shore   22

Rain Falls, It Dries Up   24

With Your Right Hand on the Back of My Head   25

In Your Arms   26

The Second Eclogue   27

Friday   29

Are You Surprised, Love   31

The Third Eclogue   32

Rainstorm   34

Only Skin and Bones and Pain   35

Autumn Begins Impatiently   38

Metaphors   40

Calendar   41

If You Listen to Me…   45

Charm   47

I Hid You   48

Couplets on a Moonlit Night   49

Spring Flies   50

Suddenly   51

Night   52

Flower Song   53

Lines at the End of October   54

Goats   55

Winter Sunlight   56

The Fourth Eclogue   57

Hesitating Ode   60

Columbus   62

Youth   63

The Terrifying Angel   64

Paris   66

The Red Flower   68

Troubled Night   69

Unnoticed   70

The Fifth Eclogue   72

I Don't Know   73

Childhood   75

They Couldn't Take It Any More   76

Pieces of Paper   78

Old Prisons   81

In a Noisy Palm Tree   82

Not Even Memory, No Magic   83

In Hiding   84

Picnic in May   85

Landscape in a Dream   86

Fragment   87

The Seventh Eclogue   88

A Letter to My Wife   90

Root   92

Like Memory (À la Recherche)   93

The Eighth Eclogue   95

Forced March   98

Postcard 1   99

Postcard 2   100

Postcard 3   101

Postcard 4   102

About Miklós Radnóti   103

IN MEMORY OF OUR FRIEND, JEFF MARKS

CLOUDED SKY

Spain, Spain

For two days it has poured like this, and as I open
my window the roofs of Paris shine,
a cloud settles on my table,
moist light blows over my face.

From above houses, standing far down in gutters,
the rain-beaten soot cries on me
and I am ashamed of this dusk, dirty
with loose mud and news.

O black-winged war, whipping us.
Terror flies across the border.
No one sows, no one reaps on the other side.
Grapes aren't picked any more.

The young bird doesn't sing, the sun doesn't
burn in the sky, mothers don't have sons
any more. Spain, only your bloody rivers
run and boil.

But new armies will come, if need be from nothingness,
like mad tornadoes,
armies starting from deep
mines and wounded fields.

Freedom, men cry about your fate!
This afternoon, they sang for you.
With heavy words, the wet-faced poor
of Paris sang about your battles.

1937

Federico García Lorca

Because Spain loved you,
because lovers read your poems,
what else could they do?
You were a poet—*they* killed you.
Now the people fight without you,
Federico García Lorca.

1937

Autumn and Death

To the memory of Etel Nagy

How many hard autumns and deaths,
what a wild list of deaths I've seen!
The smell of incense always mixes
with the smell of rotting leaves.

Mixes? No, it leans forward and runs
before the snow covers it.
The two smells are squat robbers
and goodbyes.

Even now dusk cradles two memories—
the passing smell of summer, falling,
and a kind, simple smell
that bent in your direction when the unfaithful sky
gave your body to the cold earth.

*

The woods grow naked,
the meadow is slippery,
seven lovely stars burn around you.
Suddenly in the ground
seven moles run whistling circles
around your body.

*

Oh, where did you come from, dancing into the light?
From the foot of a wall? From deep wet darkness?
What wings lifted you?
What signal did you see in the sky?

What happened to you,
body hunted by a soul,
flying and hammering!
Candle flames and a new breath
dance instead of you now, for you now.

What happened to you, body hunted by a soul,
hammering and flying?
You were light as air once,
now you're heavy as a stone.

The earth hides you.
Not like a squirrel inside a tree,
not like seeds in black earth,
not just for the winter—
Forever. Hidden like your memory
in this poem.

     1939

At an Impatient Hour

I lived high in the air, in the wind, where the sun was.
Hungary, now you lock up your broken son in valleys!
   You dress me in shadows, and in the evening landscape
   the sunset's fire doesn't comfort me.

Rocks above me, the white sky far away,
I live in the depths among mute stones.
   Maybe I should be silent too. What makes me
   write poems today? Tell me, is it death? Who asks,

Who asks about life,
and about this poem—mere fragments?
   Know that there won't even be one cry,
   that they won't bury you, that the valley won't hold you.

The wind will scatter you. But before long
a stone will echo
   what I say, and young men and young women,
   grown tall, will understand it.

    January 10, 1939

Thursday

In a cheap New York hotel
T tied a rope around his neck.
He walked around homeless for many years.
How can he go on?

In Prague JM killed himself,
a stranger in his own country,
and PR hasn't written anything in a year.
Maybe he sleeps under a dead root.

Fog drifted down on his eyes. It was
sadness. In Spain. This man who wrote poems
wanted to be free. How can he
shout at the blinding edge of a knife?

How can he shout at eternity
if his road ends at the end?
How can the homeless or chained
demand life?

When lambs bite
and whispering doves live on raw meat,
when snakes whistle on the road
and the wind screeches and flies.

May 6, 1939

For an Edition of *The Steep Road*

I am a poet and no one needs me.
Even when I grumble without words
U–U–U– it doesn't matter. Insulting
devils sing, I don't.

Believe me, believe me, there's good reason
why suspicion keeps me going!
I am a poet whose works are burned.
I am a witness to the truth.

I am the one who knows snow is white,
blood and the poppy red,
the poppy's delicate, flaxen stem is green.

I am the one they'll kill finally,
because I myself never killed.

June 1, 1939

Early Summer

1

I sit in a small meadow. The grass reaches up to my shoulder,
it whispers and sways. A butterfly drifts past.
My sadness whispers and dissolves. Thin dust flies
up to the sun from the road.

The grass sits down too, a bright wind pushes it.
The sky's blue wrinkles above me.
Small noises and small things blow
between the trees I walked past, writing a poem.

2

Words touch my face: milkweed,
I whisper, and you, sparkling primrose,
St. George's flower, St. Peter's key,
color waving on the edge of the ditch!

And if you wither, others will take your place,
Sweet William comes, a tiny flash!

3

I stand up, the meadow stands with me.
The wind has died down, a primrose winks.
I start off and on the other side
dwarf-pears' falling petals
cry there's no mercy anyway.

4

But instead others come. I leave
and others take my place. Is this all there is?
Just as a bird forgets the star-shaped
prints its delicate feet leave in the snow . . . .

It's amazing how much like winter preparing for summer is!
And now the summer crackles again.

A bush moves and a shaft of sunlight carries
the terrified feather of a small bird.

June 4, 1939

Song

Whipped by sorrow now
each day I walk
exiled in my own country

and it barely matters how long or where.
I come, go, sit,
and even the distant stars
come down and attack me.

Even the distant stars
hide behind clouds.
I stumble through the night
to the shores where reeds grow.

Where reeds grow
nobody walks with me now
and I haven't really wanted
to dance for a long time.

For a long time the deer
with its chilly nose hasn't followed me.
I wade through a swamp,
mist curls up from its surface,

mist curls up from its surface
and I sink, and sink.
Above me, a pair of
hawks hang like wet rags.

June 7, 1939

Love Poem

Up there, in the white ragged sky
the sun stands heavy.
Then it waves coldly and leaves.
here, in your eyes, weak grainy sunlight
drizzles, and the blue pierces it.
The path runs yellow.
For a long time weeds have covered it.

Because autumn is here. Walnuts are shaken out of the trees.
And in rooms silence drips from the walls.
Let the small dove, dreaming on your shoulder, fly away.
The leaf falls, frost approaches,
the stiff meadow topples. You hear the quiet plunging.

O soft guardian of the seasons, how I love you!
And love you.

October 2, 1939

Two Fragments

1.

The evening splashed down and the high trees
swam away in it. Behind the fog
the waking Great Bear growled.

It grew dark. I don't see you here
although you stand beside me under this branch
then fly up, opening your wings.

You don't have a body now. Are you an angel?
You leave me here, but it doesn't matter. I know you'll be back.
Don't you even have a body now? The fog drizzles on you too,
turning the hair on your forehead gray.

2.

And like brown coal rooted in the deepest mines
the branch hides in the fog,
bending occasionally, leaving one or two cool
dark drops on my face.

Think—the other side of the fog! I shiver,
I should be happy, now that the world is bandaged with fog
and I see nothing. Nothing?

For no reason the clean smell of mushrooms, everything
there is, comforts me. O God,
the fog curls around me! For no reason.

I stand in the cool rotting leaves
among my unwinding visions.

November 23, 1939

Fires

Fires break out and slowly die forever.
Soldiers' ghosts fly to the bright meridians. One soul!
Oh, it doesn't matter who this one or that one was
while the heat bends repeatedly here, and the frost screams there.
Sailors at the guns of torn ships, drunk on homesickness,
vomit in their yellow fear.
Mines burst everywhere, death watches carefully,
and sometimes at high tide, with a slippery body, it crawls ashore.
Dead men follow it. Dolphins are ripped apart.
Dawn wakes too but no one needs it.
A plane roars across. Its shadow
follows it silently on the fox-eyed sea.
A whirlpool breathes, signals cross on the water,
blood flowers on the reef instead of coral,
the plague howls all day, oil leaks over the fire engines,
insanity and fear hide behind them.
Then the sun drowns in smoke and, like a long-stemmed pain,
the moon bends repeatedly on the other side
and fires break out, and slowly die forever.
Soldiers' ghosts fly to the bright meridians.

December 20, 1939

Simple-Minded Song About My Wife

The door rattles when she steps in,
flowerpots click
and in her hair a small dreamy blond streak
chirps like a panicky sparrow.

The old wire lightcord squawks too,
brushing its awkward body against her.
Everything spins. I can't even write about it.

She has come back. She has been gone all day.
There is the large petal of a poppy in her hand.
She'll chase death away with it.

January 5, 1940

Like Death

Silence squats on my heart, slow darkness covers me.
The ice clicks quietly. Along the forest road
the river crackles, its surface stops flowing, painfully,
and stabs at the shore.

How long will winter last? Underground, the bones of beautiful
lovers from the past are cold, and crack.
In the lap of its deep cave, the bear's coat bristles. The small
deer moans and cries.

The small deer cries, there's lead in the winter sky,
fringes of clouds blow apart, cold darkness blows,
the moon flashes now and then, a snow-white monster flies
around shaking the trees.

Slowly, frost toys with the air, and like death, a serious,
weak flower of ice snaps on the windowpane.
You think it's lace but it dissolves and runs down
like sweat.

This is how this poem walks up to you—
the words stamp quietly, then they fly up and crash,
just like death. And afterwards, silence
*whish*es, listens.

February 27, 1940

Clouded Sky

The moon hangs on a clouded sky.
I am surprised that I live.
Anxiously, with great care, death looks for us
and those it finds are all terribly white.

Sometimes a year looks back and howls
then drops to its knees.
Autumn is too much for me. It waits again
and winter waits with its dull pain.

The forest bleeds. The hours bleed.
Time spins overhead,
the wind scrawls
big dark numbers on the snow.

But I am still here
and I know why and why the air feels heavy—
a warm silence brimming with tiny noises circles me
just as it was before my birth.

I stop at the foot of a tree.
Its leaves yell with anger.
A branch reaches down. Is it strangling me?
I am not a coward. I am not weak, I am

tired. And silent. And the branch
is mute and afraid as it enters my hair.
I should forget it, but I
forget nothing.

Clouds pour across the moon. Anger
leaves a poisonous dark-green bruise on the sky.
I roll myself a cigarette,
slowly, carefully. I live.

June 8, 1940

Maybe . . .

Maybe if I were a child again . . .
or could go crazy.

The world getting bigger and bigger . . .
then I would play and float,
then the sun would blaze again,
then the distance would explode with light.

The net of logic opens
and shuts again.

*

I would be a child, but memory hurts.
Nettles sting like splinters in my tiny fingers.
And leaves grow high on the mulberry tree.

Or maybe I could be a nice madman
and live in a yellow house high among yellow
flowers, a small bell tied around my neck . . . .

But I just look around. The ditch is here.
I walk and think and stand, then walk again.
And wait for longer and longer winters.

Palinode

But don't leave me, delicate mind!
   Don't let me go crazy.
Sweet wounded reason, don't
   leave me now.

Don't leave me. Let me die, without fear,
   a clean lovely death,
like Empedocles, who smiled as he fell
   into the crater.

July 12, 1940

In My Memories

Flowers pacing in my memories,
I stand in the flapping rain.
Two women come with moist flashing teeth,
  then two doves. Their fat
breasts brush the ground.

A whole year already! One mild rainy evening,
on the road toward Senlis, I was happy again
for a minute in an odd way.
  There were green walls around me,
silent ferns kept bending

and from Ermenonville slender young
birches ran up to us like silly
girls in white skirts, and where the road turned
  a soldier stood on a ripple
of shining mud, a rose in his mouth.

Like light shooting across the sky—
Gyula and gentle Susan sat facing me.
Fanny was beside me too. The landscape moved
  in her blue eyes and above our heads
the playful mane of the motorcar flapped.

The Paris we loved expected us for the evening.
Since then quick death roared past there too
gathering a bunch of brilliant flowers.
  There's blood on the birches. They are
ashamed and wander among the warm bodies of the dead,

and the soldier, a hero now, a tenant of cold holes,
lies on his back and the rose grows out of his heart.
His country burns. Cemeteries think and rock
    in the flames.
Trees doubled by cramps, walls everywhere, sweating.

Overhead the gritty sky still burns,
the stars still come out each evening
and with tears of dew dawns race
    toward the silent sun.
Would the landscape speak if I asked it something?

Flowers pacing in my memories,
I stand in the flapping rain.
An army of women and children walks down the road.
    Smoke in the sky,
a cloud's ripple. It's lifting. Light. Silver.

1940

Red Shore

The road has grown silent, a crow
wobbles across it like a pregnant woman.
"Well crow, finally!" the road sighs,
and babbles about its grief.

In the ground, wounded seeds listen.
The battlescarred landscape's eyelashes flicker—
even though the evening rocks it more and more
gently now, it still hasn't forgotten.

A small mine hides in a small hole,
glitters angrily, wants to explode,
but it's afraid. Cabbages stare
at it darkly and hold it down.

There at the foot of a young tree,
behind the sunflowers hanging their wise heads,
a steel-blue fog stretches across in straight lines—
thick barbed wire waits for blood.

But at dawn, when dew weighs it down
(its stem is a delicate fuse),
carefully the golden squash
blossom creeps through the wire and opens.

And soon, silence drizzles again.
Sometimes a stork stands on top of a trench.
Florian plows over the approach trenches
that are rabbit holes now.

The workers come back.
Weavers weave again.
They dream about fine thread
until the crystals of dawn wake them.

Women bend down again and again,
a new world grows at their feet.
Vain little girls in dresses red as poppies
and boys, like little butting goats, make noise.

And soaked in the bearded light of the stars,
the wise order of the world returns,
the order of animals and ears of corn,
of gentle service regulations.

January 17, 1941

Rain Falls, It Dries Up

Rain falls. It dries up. The sun shines. A horse whinnies.
Just look at the little ripples of the world.

A lamp burns in the back of the shop, a cat wails.
Girls sew and giggle, their fingernails are cloudy.

They eat pickles. Their shrill scissors clatter.
They forget that Monday and Tuesday were the same.

There's a man around the corner who sells perfume.
I know his wife from the way she smells.

The one before was senile, died, was forgotten
like everybody else, like the system for finding square roots.

They forget well. Yesterday's dead
are neatly frozen in their hearts.

A newspaper page flaps in the wind; it turns into a paper hat.
They forgot a poet too. I know him. He's still alive.

He still goes to coffeehouses. Now and then I see him,
the shoulders of his dark suit are speckled with dandruff.

What else should I write in this poem? Maybe I'll let it drop
the way a sycamore sheds a leaf.

They'll forget it anyway. Nothing helps.
Just look at the little ripples of the world.

January 30, 1941

With Your Right Hand on the Back of My Head

I lay at night with your right hand on the back of my head,
daytime still hurt because I asked you not to take it away.
I listened to the blood circling in your neck.

It was around twelve and sleep weighed on me,
it fell as suddenly as it did years ago, in
my drowsy, woolly childhood, and it rocked me as gently.

You tell me that it wasn't even three o'clock
when I woke, afraid, and sat up
and mumbled and recited poems and howled incoherently.

I spread my arms out the way a bird ruffled by fear
beats its wings when a shadow curves in the garden.
I was planning to go, but where? Terrified by what kind of death?

Dear, you tried to quiet me and I, sleeping as I sat, let you.
I lay back silently. The road of terrors waited.
And I kept on dreaming. Maybe about a different death.

April 6,1941

In Your Arms

I sleep in your arms,
it's quiet.
You sleep in my arms,
it's quiet.
I'm a child in your arms
who is silent.
You're a child in my arms.
I listen.
You hold me in your arms
when I'm afraid.
I hold you in my arms.
I'm not afraid.
In your arms even the great silence
of death can't
scare me.
In your arms I'll
survive death.
It's a dream.

April 20, 1941

The Second Eclogue

Pilot:

We went pretty far last night. I was so angry I laughed.
Fighters buzzed me like a swarm of bees.
They had good protection. Friend, you should have seen how they
      fired.
Finally another one of our squadrons appeared on the horizon.
I barely missed getting shot down, pieces of me swept up down
      below.
But I'm back you see. And tomorrow I'll shiver with fear again
and a horrified Europe will hide in its cellars from me—
Oh forget it, I've had enough. Did you write again today?

Poet:

Yes, I wrote. What else can I do? Poets write, cats wail, dogs howl,
small fish coyly scatter their eggs. I write about everything.
I even write for you, so you'll know I'm alive.
I write when the light of the bloodshot moon stumbles
among the exploding, collapsing rows of houses,
when parks are torn up, when breathing stops,
when even the sky vomits, and the planes keep coming.
They disappear, then swoop down again like the roar of madness!
I write. What else can I do? And a poem is very dangerous,
if you only knew how sensitive, how unpredictable even one line is!
You need bravery for all this, you see. Poets write, cats
wail, dogs howl, and small fish—
and so on— But what do you know? You listen to the plane
and your ear hums with the noise even when you can't hear it.
Don't deny it, the plane's your friend. It's part of you.
What are you thinking about when you fly over us?

Pilot:

You can laugh but I'm scared up there. I close my eyes and think
about my girl, about lying in bed down here.
Or I only sing about her, between my teeth, quietly,
in the crazy uproar of the steaming soldiers' club.
Up there, I want to come down. Down here, I want to fly again.
There's no place on earth for me.
And I know the airplane means too much to me,
but up there the rhythm of our pain is the same—
You know what I mean! You'll write about it. It won't be a secret
any more that I, who only destroy now, lived like a man too,
homeless between the earth and the sky. O God, who will
        understand—
Will you write about me?

Poet:

If I'm alive. If there's anyone left.

   April 27, 1941

Friday

April is crazy.
The sun won't come out.
I drank for a week
and only got more sober.

April is crazy.
Its frost whips you.
Somebody writes, and each week
sells out his country.

April is crazy.
Snow covers everything and creaks.
Many have run away
and it cracked their hearts.

April is crazy.
It whines over the frost.
Three of my friends have left
and all three are lost.

April is crazy.
Sometimes a wild rain falls.
One man is insane and doesn't
even know what happened.

April is crazy.
Many rivers are flooded.
The second died
with two bullets in his brain.

Four days ago they killed him.
The third is a prisoner.
Frost pinches the fruit off.
A smile circles my mouth.

I hear, "Take care of yourself.
That's how you'll pay them back!"

May 18, 1941

Are You Surprised, Love

Are you surprised, love, that I'm so thin?
The trouble of worlds is heavy, the trouble of worlds hurts me.
Up there, the mountains try to bring something into the world,
passes collapse, and here in this valley, walls crack.
Tomorrow evening, small blond cows won't find
their mild stables, they'll cry until morning
while farmers lie hidden in filthy ditches,
while meaningless order and death rule.
Pale women sit by themselves like orphans
in forests, under trees, on strange porches,
under a cool moon, quietly waiting to see their own blood,
and feel their stomachs turn.
They sing and gather like angels.
Oh, if I could only believe I'm crazy,
on fire, battered by my obsessions,
but there's war, you see, and afterwards only rubble and scum
left. It barely matters whether I live or die.
Dreams don't comfort me, dawns fall,
they all find me wide awake. I get thinner that way.
Light vibrates inside my tired eyes
but I still smile sometimes. I smile because
even seeds hiding in the earth are happy when they've outlived
another winter. I think about you, love, and love,
a sleepy mood, walks like a tiger and toys with me.

May 20, 1941

The Third Eclogue

Shepherd Muse, come to me here, even though I sit in
a sleepy café. Light flashes outside, moles dig silently
in the fields, small humps grow on the earth.
Fishermen with strong, brown bodies and white teeth, their work
done before daybreak, sleep in the oily hulls of their boats.

Shepherd Muse, come to me here in this city grove.
Even these seven noisy salesmen shouldn't scare me away,
believe me, these poor men have their worries even here—
and look at all those lawyers, not one plays the flute
any more, instead they puff on big cigars!

Come to me here! I was teaching and ran in here between classes
to think about the magic of love, on the wings of all this smoke.
I thought I'd be like a dead tree brought back to life
by the zany little song of a bird, and I rose
to the old heights, the wild desires of youth.

Shepherd Muse, help me! All the trumpets of dawn scream
about her now! In a deep, foggy voice they sing about her figure,
how her body shines, how an awkward smile lights up in her eyes,
how a sigh starts with clever dance steps on her lips,
how she moves, how she embraces, how she looks at the moon!

Shepherd Muse, help me! Let me sing about love now.
Sadness claws at me all the time, new pains chase me
through the world, always new ones! Soon I will die here.
Trees grow crooked, the mouths of salt mines cave in,
a brick screams in the wall— This is what I dream.

Shepherd Muse, help me! Oh, how poets die in this age—
The sky collapses on us, there are no hills to mark our ashes,
no fine, exquisitely shaped Greek urns to guard them, only a
poem or two, if there are any left at all— Can I still write about
        love?
Her body shines for me, O Shepherd Muse, help me!

June 12, 1941

Rainstorm

You escape just in time! The stream is heavy with sadness.
The wind gets ruffled. Clouds break.
Torrents of rain slam into the water.
Drops crumble. I follow you with my eyes.

Drops crumble. But my body reaches out
toward you, the strong web of my muscles
remembers your wild embrace, your love,
and is tortured by sadness.

My body is tortured by sadness over you,
my soul flies after you to meet you.
Nothing, nothing, not even this rainstorm
will wash away my desire for you.

July 2, 1941

Only Skin and Bones and Pain

On the death of Babits Mihály

1

After so much suffering
your cold brown body rests.
It's only skin and bones and pain.
Like a broken tree
showing its rings of age
it shows your tortured years.
It's only skin and bones and pain
like this country.
Patron Saint Blaise, hold him!
O requiem aeternam dona ei . . . Domine!

2

Painful words rise into my mouth like drops of foam,
come, stand around him!
Stumbling from my
grief-stricken mind
don't betray me.
Weep on his grave,
clods of earth!
Transparent *shroud*,
cover him.
Clanging *bell*, toll for him,
betrayed long ago by sounds.
Soaring *soul*, round *pearl*,
distant *star*, lazy-eyed *moon*,
mourn for him, mourn . . .

3

For many years, we've had no hope:
cancer tore you apart. The eternal texture
of a distant world shone in your eyes,
and you were becoming ageless like the stars.

We knew you were dying. When you left
only your work, we were like orphans.
Our hearts beat faster. We were inspired,
afraid and dizzy at your heights.

4

Who will watch our hands now when we write?
Sick, tired, you were our model.
Who will create our standards now?
Look how pain broke
this poem into fragments.

What would *you* say?—Your work
is the only measure now
for poets taking their first, hestitating steps.

No one understands why we feel like orphans.
We nod: "Yes, he's dead—"
to those who didn't know you,
didn't sit by your bed, your table.

They won't know what hurt us.
They won't ask, nobody will ask them
the password we've used
for so many years: "Who's seen him?
Tell me, how's Babits Mihály?"

5

His hand won't hold a pen.
His eyes won't see the night anymore.
Eternal light, fire in the sky,
shines on him through the smoke of the world.

August-September, 1941

Autumn Begins Impatiently

From between wild iron-gray flags
the sun billows impatiently,
its gases rush and bend. Streaming away,
light cuts into the lowering fog.

The clouds are ruffled, the wind ripples
the mirror of the sky, the blue flies away.
A low-flying swallow writes
a screaming word and gets away.

Autumn begins impatiently.
The rust on the branches swings up and down,
the sky's breath is cool.
The sky warms nothing, it smokes,
and today the sun only sighs.

A lizard scuttles along the walls of big graveyards
and the hungry madness of
autumn wasps, hungry for sugar, buzzes and glows.

Men sit on the banks
of ditches, watching
the deep fires of death.
The smell of heavy leaf-mold sails over.

Fire darts on the road,
flapping—half light, half blood.
The fiery brown leaf
flaps in the wind.

Clusters are heavy, vine-shoots wither,
the stems of yellow flowers
crackle, seeds drop from the corn.

The meadow swims in the evening fog
and the mad rattle of distant wagons
shakes the remaining
leaves from the trees.

The countryside falls asleep.
Death is white,
it soars gracefully, the sky
cradles the garden.
Look—in your hair—a gold autumn leaf!
Above you, a branch cried.

Oh, flame up in autumn over death
and lift me with your love.
Be thoughtful now so I can love you
and kiss you. Be hungry, for dreams.

Love me joyfully, don't go away, drift
with me into the dark sky of our dreams.
Sleep. The thrush sleeps in the tree,
the walnut falls on the moist leafy soil
and doesn't make a sound. Reason falls apart.

October 10, 1941

Metaphors

You are like a whispering branch
when you bend over me,
or like the secret taste
of a poppy—

and like ripples continually forming in time
you excite me,
and quiet me
like stone on top of a grave.

You are like a friend I grew up with,
and even today I don't really know
the smell
of your thick hair.

Sometimes when you look sad, I'm afraid
you'll leave me, like
coiled drifting smoke, and sometimes when
you're the color of lightning, I'm afraid of you—

like the exploding sky, when the sun
burns it dark gold.
And when you're angry, you
are like the letter "u,"

deep-voiced, vibrating again and again.
Dark. At times like these
I draw smiles
like bright nooses around you.

November 16, 1941

Calendar

January

The sun rises late. The sky is
filled with a darkness
so black
it almost spills over.
In the gray cold, dawn
steps on the ice and cracks it.

February 5, 1941

February

The snow flutters, settles to the ground,
then melts; cutting a path,
it trickles away.
The sun flashes. The sky flashes.
The sun blinks.
Outside, in a white voice,
the flock talks to it.
A sparrow shakes its feathers in that direction and sings.

February 21, 1941

March

Look—goose-pimples on a puddle!
March walks
under the trees with wild,
happy winds.
The buds haven't come out, they're afraid
of the cold, spiders aren't weaving their webs,
only little chickens roll around
like balls of yellow gold.

February 26, 1941

April

A breeze cries out. It steps on a tiny piece of glass
and hops away on one leg.
O April, April,
the sun doesn't shine. Tiny buds,
noses always wet, don't open
when the sky fills with whistling.

    March 12, 1939

May

A petal shivers in the tree and falls.
White smells come with evening.
A chilly night pours over the mountain.
Rows of leafy trees walk in it.
The little warmth there is hides from the cold.
The candles on wild chestnut trees shine.

    February 25, 1941

June

Look around, it is noon now, you'll see a miracle.
The sky is bright, its brow smooth.
Along the roads the acacias bloom.
Suddenly there are gold crests on little streams.
A fat, bragging, lazy dragonfly
with a diamond body writes
glittering signs in the bright air.

    February 28, 1941

July

Up there, the clouds are so angry their bellies ache,
they make faces.
Rainstorms run around barefoot
with their hair all wet.
They get tired, they hide in the ground,
night falls.
The clean body of heat sits above
the bright faces of the trees.

June 12, 1940

August

The meadow soaks in the
blaring light of the sun.
A pretty golden apple
yellows among the leaves.
A red squirrel yelps and up in the proud
wild chestnut tree the thorns are sharp.

July 21, 1940

September

How many Septembers have I lived to think about
lilies and the brown jewel wild chestnuts lie
under the trees. They remind you of Africa's
scorching heat before a cool rain.
Evening makes its bed among the clouds
and a dim light spills over the tired trees.
Sweet Autumn shows up with her hair down.

July 15, 1940

October

The wind is golden and cool.
The wanderers sit down.
A mouse is dressing in the dark shed.
Above me a branch shines like gold.
Everything is gold here.
The corn, brought here across the Atlantic,
waves its ripped yellow flags,
afraid of losing them.

  February 7, 1941

November

Frost has come, it screams on the wall.
The teeth of the dead click. You can hear it.
Up in the dry brown tree,
gray, bushy wild myrtles rustle.
A baby owl is dropping its prophecies on me.
Am I afraid? Maybe I'm not afraid?

  January 14, 1939

December

At 12 the sun is a silver moon,
a dream of itself on the sky.
The fog drifts like a sluggish bird.
Snow falls during the night and
an angel glides through the darkness.
Death steps noiselessly
over deep snow.

  February 11, 1941

If You Listen to Me . . .

On the windowpane my breath
leaves a mist. It fades quickly.
A blurred moon grows in it
as I question myself.
Can anything help me?
My love tied into knots
glows like pain
and breaks me out of my sleep every night.

In the inside left pocket of my coat,
just above the heart, there's a clean pen.
My gloom is smoke on the summer sky.
Looking up, I ask who thinks about me now,
who answers? My home is inside me.
I stand by the window here, at home,
like a sailor whose tattooed body
hangs on a wave-bitten reef.

The sky flows blue above me.
Since before dawn today, the sadness
of wet umbrellas has drizzled inside me.
The sun shines uselessly,
depressing, like a two-day beard.

The well of sadness is dark like ice.
But the sky still throbs on its surface.
This is how blue puts its good hands
in front of my buried life.
This is how sadness still gives me to the sky.

(And it doesn't last long. If you listen to me,
soon you'll hear a voice in the sky.
After the last word is spoken, talk about
how terror cracked my ribs.)

    January 15, 1942

Charm

With quivering eyes
I sit in the light
a rosetree jumps
over the hedge
the light jumps too
clouds gather
lightning
and high up
thunder
answers
thunder bellows
down into the blue
lakes wither
the surfaces flood
come into the house
take off your dress
it's raining outside
take off your shirt
let the rain wash
our hearts into one heart.

February 1, 1942

I Hid You

I hid you for a long time
the way a branch hides its
slowly ripening fruit among leaves
and like a flower of sane ice
on a winter window
you open in my mind.
Now I know what it means
when your hand swoops up to your hair.
In my heart I keep
the small tilt of your ankle too
and I'm amazed by the delicate curve
of your ribs, but coldly,
like someone who has lived
such breathing miracles.
Still, in my dreams,
I often have a hundred arms
and like a god in a dream
I hold you in those arms.

February 20, 1942

Couplets on a Moonlit Night

The moon drips on the crosses of windows,
wild-haired cats are puny devils.

The light on the rooftop is a gold casing.
Brooding tomcats.

Cautiously, they come, dragging their paws.
There are seven dogs, but a hundred bark in the distance.

Rasping, screaming, like a machine without oil,
the scared dogs whine overhead.

They don't understand what this pain is for
or why light blossoms on the walls of houses.

They don't understand—a dog doesn't understand anything—
when there's a bit more blood on the moon.

A cat is different. Satisfied by a cat,
he hunts shadows until dawn.

February 25, 1942

Spring Flies

Foreword to the Eclogues

Ice skims the river, the shores turn dark in patches.
Snow melts. The first rays of the sun splash
in puddles formed by the footprints of rabbit and deer.
With her hair untied, spring flies over the tops
of lazy mountains, at the bottom of tunnels, inside mole hills.
She runs over the roots of trees, near the arch in a bud's soft armpit,
she rests on the stems of fragile leaves, then she runs off.
Everywhere in the meadow, at the top of the hill, over rippling lakes,
    the sky flares blue.

With her hair untied, spring flies, but the angel of freedom
doesn't fly next to her now. She sleeps far below, frozen
in yellow mud, knocked out, between unconscious roots.
She sees no light, no troops of small green leaves
curling up on the shrubs. It's no use, the angel won't wake up.
She's a prisoner. The coiled black sadness of prisoners
drips in her dreams and the soil, the freezing night, weigh down
her heart. She dreams. Even her sighs don't move her breasts.
    The ice doesn't crack below.

Roots, leaves, dogs, fish, horses, bulls, sleepers, wake up!

April 11, 1942

Suddenly

Suddenly at night the wall moves,
silence breaks into the heart, and the word breaks out.
The rib twinges. Familiar with grief, the pulse under the bone fades.
Silently the body rises. Only the wall is heard.
And the heart, the hand and the mouth know that this is death,
       this is death.
This is prison when the lights fade.
Inside the convicts know, outside the guards know too
that the current all comes together in one body.
The lightbulb is quiet, a shadow dashes through the cell,
and then the guards, the convicts and the bugs smell the odor
of scorched human flesh.

    April 20, 1942

Night

The heart sleeps, and fear sleeps in the heart.
The fly sleeps near the cobweb on the wall.
It is quiet in the house,
the wakeful mouse is quiet,
the garden sleeps, the branch,
the woodpecker in the tree,
the bee in the hive, the chafer in the rose.
Summer sleeps in the spinning grains of wheat,
fire sleeps in the moon.
A cold medal hangs in the sky.
Autumn wakes. It steals through the night.

June 1, 1942

Flower Song

Above you, an apple branch.
Petals fall on your lips,
a few late ones trickle down
into your hair and eyes.

All day I look at your mouth.
Branches bend to your eyes.
Light skims their light,
a spirit waking to be kissed.

It disappears. You shut your eyes.
A frail petal plays its
shadow over the lashes,
darkness from somewhere.

Darkness, but don't be afraid.
The dumb silver night will speak.
The branch in the sky will blossom.
The moon stares at this crippled world.

Nagyvárad, Military Hospital
August 25, 1942

Lines at the End of October

A stream with a wavy bed and a white smile runs down the
    mountainside,
an autumn leaf hops around, swims away on a crest.
Look—in the shade a dogwood's twisted jewel flashes on a bush
and grassblades sparkle in the light and shake like old people.
The sun still shines, but it's so ripe now that only its calm wisdom
keeps it from falling out of the sky. It worries about its gold.
I'm slow too and wise in this slow and wise brightness.
I worry and want to protect you from winter cold. Blind thoughts
of firewood, of heavy clothes, come and go in your eyes,
like a breath your drowsy sorrow grazes their film and floods
the blue glare. A sentence goes to sleep on your mouth,
a kiss wakes. The snow blackens, winter. The corners
of the big autumn sky are black now, the tracks dawn
left are slippery. Come sleep under the
long beard of night. Look—I'm your
grown-up son, your lover, old enough for my portion of our troubles,
for more than just writing poems. We'll be lying in the dark and with
a night ear I'll listen and wait; like a young stork
learning to fly in autumn, tripping over itself,
I roll around on the wide couch. Slowly I fly away, crying Oh!
I take on your troubled thoughts and their pulse rocks me to sleep.
We two sleep with one thought. Until a dream stops us we hear
the moist dark flag of autumn lashing through the night.

Élesd-Nagytelekmajor
September 28–November 14, 1942

Goats

Fog blurs the colors
in the clouds.
Darkness grows in the grass.
The soft little bodies of
fattening goats glow
in the dark.

A gray one stands by herself.
The light on her fur fades,
dreams flit across her eyes,
her udder bulges
with sun-ripened grass
and she stares past the quiet stable.

Dusk scatters its vapors
in the air, and the blood spilled
along the edge of the sky flares up.
A lecherous buck bites off
flowers and, standing on his hind legs,
laughs at the moon.

Another walks like a ghost
treading softly through the short grass.
He cries in a hollow wooden voice.
His beard shakes. He scatters
bunches of little, dark, round droppings
through the night

Nagytelekmajor
November 12, 1942

Winter Sunlight

The melting snow collapses
and trickles away in all directions.
Steaming kettles turn
purple like baked pumpkins.

An icicle stretches.
Its drops are heavy.
A few puddles form
and look at the sky, timidly.

And there, on a shelf in the sky,
the snow slides back a little.
I'm a man of few words now,
I almost never argue.

Am I waiting just for lunch
or for death too?
Will I fly like a soul,
bruising the night and the day?

My shadow looks at me, until
the winter sun broods.
I have a cap issued by the government.
On the sun's head there's a hat.

December 26, 1942

The Fourth Eclogue

Poet:

If you had only asked me when I was an infant—
O then, then I knew!
I howled. "I don't want the world! It's cruel!"
Now darkness hits me like a club and light cuts into me!
But I survived. My head's been hard for a long time,
and my lungs only got stronger from all the crying.

Voice:

Red waves of scarlet fever
and measles washed you ashore.
Once a lake tried to swallow you but it spat you out.
What do you think, why did time take you in its arms?
And your heart, your liver, your winglike lungs,
this sloppy, wet, mysterious machine,
how does it work—why? And that scary flower,
cancer, has it blossomed in your flesh?

Poet:

I was born. I protested. And I'm still here.
I grew up. You ask me why. Well, I don't know.
I always wanted to be free
and guards led me down the road.

Voice:

You've been to blinding peaks, polished by the wind,
you've seen tame deer kneeling among
withered bushes on a mountain at night.
You've seen drops of resin on the sunlit trunk of a tree,
and a young, naked woman rising out of the river,
once a large beetle landed on your hand—

Poet:

You don't see any of these in prison.
I could have been a mountain, a plant, a bird—
a comforting, butterfly thought,
a passing curse. Help me, freedom,
let me find my home at last!

The peaks again, the woods, the woman and the bushes,
the wings of the soul that burn in the wind!
To be born again, into a new world,
where the sun rises in new dawns and
its light bursts from its yellow gases.

It's quiet now, but the breath of a storm
is in the air, ripe fruit sway on the branches.
A light wind carries the flying moth.
Death blows among the trees.

And I know I'm ripe for death,
the waves of time that lifted are dropping me now.
I was a prisoner and my loneliness
grows slowly like the crescent moon.

I will be free, the earth will let go of me
and above the earth, the shattered world will glide
on the wind. The writing tablets have cracked.
Imagination, fly, rise high on your heavy wings!

Voice:

The fruit sways. When it's ripe it falls.
The deep earth crowded with memories will calm you.
But let the smoke of your anger rise,
and if everything else is broken, write on the sky!

March 15, 1943

Hesitating Ode

I've been planning to tell you
about the secret galaxy of my love for so long—
in just one image, just the essence.
But you are swarming and flooding inside me like
existence, as eternal and certain sometimes
as a snail shell changed to stone inside a stone.
Spattered by the moon, night curves over my head
and hunts for the dreams that rustle
suddenly, then take flight. But I still can't
tell you what it really means to me when I write
and feel your warm glance above my hands.
Metaphors are useless. They come up. I drop them.
And tomorrow I'll begin the whole thing over again
because I'm worth about as much as the words
in this poem and because all this excites me until
I'm only bone and a few tufts of hair.
You are tired. I feel it too. It was a long day.
What else can I say? Objects look at each other
and praise you, half a cube of sugar sings
on the table, drops of honey fall and
glow on the tablecloth like beads of pure gold.
An empty glass clinks by itself,
happy because it lives with you. And maybe I'll
have time to tell you what it's like when it waits
for you to come back. Dreaming's slowly falling
darkness touches, touches me, flies off, then touches
your brow again. Your heavy lids say goodbye.
Your hair spreads out and flickers
and you sleep. The long shadow of your eyelashes
quivers. Your hand sinks on

my pillow, a birch branch going to sleep.
But I sleep in you also. You aren't "another" world.
And I can hear how the many mysterious,
thin, wise lines change

                        in your cool palm.

May 26, 1943

Columbus

He has no time to write now in the journal he began long ago
with the words: *In Nomine Domini Jesu Christi.*
Wind turns the pages. He doesn't touch it. He thinks of other things.
An insane frozen sky with big claws purrs above him.

Columbus stands with his legs apart in the night.
Four mutineers huddle near the foot of the mast.
The large ship rolls, the sails sing in the wind.

Maybe Rodrigo is wrong?—His throat swells.
But don't those clumps of grass mean land is near?
I myself saw a flock of birds fly west,
and yesterday a dove.
                              "Land! Land!" someone yells.
It was two o'clock on a dark Friday morning.
Laudetur. They all mumbled and stood there, holding their hats.
    June 1, 1943

Youth

When Columbus stepped onto the noisy beach
trailed by his drunken sailors,
a fragrant wind started to blow, a nest fell at his feet,
a green monkey, shaking its fists, ran up to him.
He felt that he knew how eternity begins.
His large eyes twinkled, his tired eyelids itched.
He shrugged and whispered something over his shoulder.

May 29, 1943

The Terrifying Angel

The terrifying angel is invisible and silent
inside me, he doesn't scream today.
But then I hear a slight noise
no louder than a grasshopper's jump.
I look around and don't see anything.
It's him. But he's cautious now. He's getting ready.
Save me, O you who love me; love me bravely.
He hides when you're here. But as soon as you leave
he's back. He swims up from the bottom of the soul,
screaming, accusing me.
This insanity works inside me like poison.
He doesn't sleep much, lives both in and outside of me,
and when the moon is out, in the white darkness,
he runs through the meadow in whistling sandals.
He searches my mother's grave and wakes her up.
"Was it worth it?" "Was it worth it?"
He whispers to her about rebellion, about giving in.
"You gave birth to him and died of it!"
Looking at me, sometimes he tears off
the pages of the calendar too soon.
"How long" and "Where to"
depend on him forever now. Last night
his words dropped into my heart
the way stones hit water,
forming rings, wobbling and spinning.
I was just going to bed, you were already asleep.
I stood there naked when he came in
and started to argue with me quietly.

There was a weird smell, his
breath chilled my ear. "Go ahead!"
he urged. "Skin shouldn't cover you.
You're raw meat and bare nerves.
Tear it off! After all, bragging about skin
is like bragging about prison,
it's crazy.
That thing all over you is merely an illusion.
Here, here's the knife.
It doesn't hurt. It only takes a second, there's only a hiss!"

And the knife woke up on the table flashing.

August 4, 1943

Paris

At the intersection of the Boulevard St. Michel
and the Rue Cujas, the sidewalk slopes a little.
Beautiful, fervent days of youth, I haven't
lost you. Your voice speaks in my heart
like an echo in a mineshaft. The baker lived
on a corner of the Rue Monsieur le Prince,

and on the left, one of the big trees
in the park was as yellow against the sky
as if it could see autumn coming.
Dear freedom, long-legged nymph,
wearing the dusk like a golden dress,
do you still hide among the misty trees?

Its drops of sweat drumming on the ground, kicking up
dust, summer marched down the road like an army.
A cool mist followed, and on both
sides smells streamed in all directions.
At noon it was still summer, but then sweet autumn
with rain on its forehead came to visit.

I lived like a child then, doing whatever I
wanted to do, and like a pedantic old man
who discovers that the world is round.
I was green but had a beard of snow.
I took walks, I didn't have any cares.
Later I descended into the hot earth.

O shouting stations, where are you?
CHÂTELET–CITÉ-ST. MICHEL–ODÉON
and DENFERT–ROCHEREAU, the one that sounds like a curse.
A map bloomed on a big stained wall.
"Oh where are you!" I cry. I listen.
The smells of bodies and ozone start rumbling.

And the nights! The long night journey
from the outskirts to the Quartier!
Will it dawn again over Paris
with strange, gray clouds?
Drunk from writing poems,
half asleep, I got undressed.

Oh, will I ever have the strength to return,
to escape the strong current of my life?
A cat from the cheap, stinking restaurant
downstairs was mating on the roof.
Will I hear that unbearable noise again?
That's where I learned what the noise must have been like
on Noah's ark as it sailed under the moon.

    August 14, 1943

The Red Flower

At night, the red flower opens
and the sunflower prays
to the dark lid of the horizon,
the cricket rubs its legs,
the bee drones in its hive
and the lark, rising and falling,
writes its sleepy lines
of evening
on the sky,
and far out in the meadow
in the dark rain,
in the path of rabbits leaping away,
grassblades huddle,
birches dressed in silver
walk through the fallen leaves.
Tomorrow, yellow autumn
will walk around here again.

August 26, 1943

Troubled Night

A duck dreamed about a hawk. Now it wakes up frightened.
It shuffles, it wiggles its tail, it stops again and again
then quacks three times and falls asleep.
But now the woolly silence is ripped apart.
An ominous wind wakes under the ragged sky
and wrinkles dreams as it runs past
the breathing sties and stables.
It prances instead of the sleeping colts.
Everything that was silent begins to whisper now.
The moon sets slowly. It swings in the
thick white odor of sleeping elderberries.

September 12, 1943

Unnoticed

You drift from youth into manhood
as unnoticed as if you were drifting off to sleep.
You have a past, you sit around facing bottles of hard liquor,
and more and more of your friends become fathers.

Now, the father comes to see you with his young son,
and pretty soon the boy understands you better,
understands the burning adventures of your heart,
and playing on the floor, together you outwit the rocking of time.

But the day comes when you make money like a grownup,
translate on commission, sell poems,
argue about contracts, calculate, protest,
and you too can only make a living with the help of "extras."

You don't look for success, you know it doesn't help.
That lady favors only those who come at the right time—
You like the poppy and the red-skinned sour cherry
instead of the honey and walnuts which fascinate sad teenagers.

And you know that in summer too a leaf can fall
no matter how much the brain burns and dances,
and that everything will be measured when you're dead.
You can't be a great athlete or a roaming sailor

but you have learned that the pen is a weapon and a tool,
and you can break your neck trying to write an honest poem
and that way too you can reach all those places
where intentions are bare and the fires of adventure burn forever.

And as you write, pressing hard on the pen, you think
about children, and there's no pride in your sad heart.
You work for them like the people in factories, creaking with
silent dust, like those in workshops who bend their backs.

November 15, 1943

The Fifth Eclogue
Fragment

To the memory of György Bálint

Dear friend, you don't know how this cold poem made me quake,
how afraid I was of words. Even today I tried to escape them.
I wrote half-lines.
                    I tried to write about other things,
but it was no use. This terrible, hidden night calls me:
"Talk about him."
                    Fear wakes me, but the voice
is silent, like the dead out there in the Ukrainian fields.
You're missing.
                    And even autumn doesn't bring news.
                                        In the forest
the promise of another furious winter whistles today. In the sky,
clouds heavy with snow fly past and halt.
Who knows if you're alive?
                            Even I don't know today. I don't shout
angrily if they wave their hands painfully and cover their faces
and don't know anything.
                        But are you alive, wounded?
Do you walk among dead leaves, circled by the thick smell of
                                                forest mud,
or are you a smell too?
                        Snow drifts over the fields.
He's missing—the news hits.
                            And inside, my heart pounds,
                                            freezes.
Between two of my ribs, a bad, ripping pain starts up,
quivers, and in my memories, words you spoke a long time ago
come back sharply and I feel your body's as real
as the dead's—
                And I still can't write about you today!

November 21, 1943

I Don't Know

I don't know what this land means to others, this little country
fenced in by fire, place of my birth,
world of my childhood, swaying in the distance.
I grew out of her like the young branch of a tree,
and I hope my body will sink down in her.
Here, I'm at home. When one by one, bushes kneel at my feet,
I know their names and the names of their flowers.
I know people who walk the roads and where they're going
and on a summer evening, I know the meaning of the pain
that turns red and trickles down the walls of houses.
This land is only a map for the pilot who flies over.
He doesn't know where the poet Vörösmarty lived.
For him factories and angry barracks can't be seen on this map.
For me there are grasshoppers, oxen, church steeples, gentle farms.
Through binoculars, he sees factories and plowed fields;
I see the worker, shaking, afraid for his work.
I see forests, orchards vibrant with song, vineyards, graveyards,
and a wizened old woman who quietly weeps and weeps among
       the graves.
The industrial plant and the railway must be destroyed.
But it's only a watchman's box and the man stands outside
sending messages with a red flag. There are children around him,
in the factory yard a sheep dog plays, rolling on the ground.
And there's the park and the footprints of lovers from the past.
Sometimes kisses tasted like honey, sometimes like blackberries.
I didn't want to take a test one day, so on my way to school
I tripped on a stone at the edge of the sidewalk.
Here is the stone, but from up there it can't be seen.
There's no instrument to show any of it.

We're sinners, just like people everywhere,
we know what we did wrong, when and how and where.
But innocent workers and poets live here too.
Knowledge grows inside nursing babies
like light. Hiding in dark cellars, they guard it,
waiting for the day when the finger of peace will leave its print
    on our land,
and their new clear words will answer our muffled ones.

Night cloud, awake, spread your great wings out over us.

January 17, 1944

Childhood

Flat on the ground, the Indian didn't move,
but up in the tree a whistling crazy force leaped around.
Wind scattered the smell of gunpowder.
On a leaf two shiny drops of blood,
on the trunk of a tree a dizzy bug doing somersaults.
Evening was a redskin. Death was heroic then.

January 25, 1944

They Couldn't Take It Any More

To the memory of Dési Huber István

So the ruined heart and lungs couldn't take it any more.
Nothing but the mind could tolerate the past,
the troubles that couldn't sleep through these psychotic years,
the faith and the disappointments.

The mind could have taken more, but the body ran away.
Your heart stopped. The paint dries,
the boxes and your canvases stay empty,
your hand doesn't pause over paper any more.

Your world and our world are deserted,
a dire, measured, wide-open world.
Bulls, horses, workers, poets cry over you,
and the Dési churches, and the Dési trees.

Without fate you became a master and
example. Faithful, true, intelligent.
Today, the time for work lifts you up,
it doesn't matter that the earth collapses on you,

workers, slow-moving people, cast you up—
this horrible ocean casts up its miraculous wreck.
You were faithful to them and they showed you no mercy,
but they'll learn, they'll never forget.

When they've learned, they'll see the places where they live,
the landscapes, their friends, the way *you* did.
It won't matter what the picture says, coffin, pitcher,
or dead wall. The message will be the same:

"Man, be careful, look at your world closely:
that was the past, this is the crazy present—
carry them in your heart. Live in this vile world
and always know what you have to do
    to change it."

    February 29, 1944

Pieces of Paper

Let Me

Let me die, love!
Make a big fire. Incinerate
me with starved flames! Burn me!
Let me die, love!

>   *April 20, 1941*

Flower

You just left. It hasn't even been five minutes.
For five minutes now you haven't been with me.

  But you see this fire
in the night, these plans. It's love,
    the imagination's
  bunch of wild flowers.

You've just left and already I want to stare at
    the blue vein above your
    ankle. I know it well.

>   *December 7, 1943*

A Little Grammar

To myself I am "I"
and to you I am "you,"
and to yourself you are "I,"
two separate powers.
Together we are "us."
But only if I say so.

>   *March 12, 1943*

Winter

A breeze scratches a leaf
frozen in the snow, and it quivers.
The clouds are like sacks
bulging with snow.
No stars. The black
trunks of the trees are huge.
The deer tracks freeze.
Wolves get ready to go down into the valley.

    February 4, 1944

The Corpse

How the corpse has grown!
His toe reaches the bedpost.
Now he is stretched out like someone
who has reached his life's goal.

Little Boy

He screams in the sunlight.
Hair of bronze, eyes of fire.
For a long time the white elephant has served
only him.

Metaphor

Are you cold? You are like the lonely
song of a bird sitting on a branch covered with snow.

Fairy Tale

In the narrow mountain cave
peace sleeps quietly.
It's still a baby.
A gentle deer nurses him daily,
a spider weaves a fine
web over the entrance to keep him safe.

Night

The body lies down but many
flickering shadows guard the walls.
The pocket watch keeps time, water
in a glass broods, the calendar is silent.

    March, 1944

Forest

A gold sword among the branches,
  sunlight cuts through.
It wounded a tree trunk
which quietly started to cry
drops of golden sap.

    1944

Old Prisons

Oh, the peace of old prisons, beautiful
   old-fashioned suffering, death,
poetic death, sublime and heroic picture,
   rhyming speech that people listen to—
how distant you are. Now, if anyone dares to move,
   he steps out into nothingness. A fog drizzles.
Reality, like a cracked pot, doesn't hold
   its shape anymore. It's waiting
to explode and scatter its worthless fragments.
   What will happen now to those who spoke in rhymes
   when they were living, allowed to live?
They uttered what is—they taught how to judge.

   Everything fallen apart, they still want to teach.
   They sit and stare, they can't do anything.

    March 27, 1944

In a Noisy Palm Tree

Most of all, I'd like to sit
in a noisy palm tree,
a soul from the sky curled up
in a shivering mortal body.

I'd sit in that tree
surrounded by wise monkeys,
the sound of their shrill voices
falling on me like a bright shower.

I'd learn their song
and sing with them.
I'd laugh, surprised
that their noses and tails
are equally blue.

The huge sun would burn
above the infested trees
and I'd be ashamed
of the human race.

The monkeys would understand—
they still have sane minds—
and maybe, living among them,
I too would get to know
the mercy of a good death.

April 5, 1944

Not Even Memory, No Magic

Like brown-skinned seeds in apple cores
so much anger lived inside my heart,
and I knew that an angel with a sword in his hand
followed, protected, and took care of me.
But if you wake up one wild day at dawn and find
everything has crumbled, and you leave like a ghost,
almost naked, losing the little you had,
then in your easygoing heart a mature,
wise, quiet humility is born.
Then, if you rebel, you speak not only for yourself, but for others,
you fight for a free future, raging like a bonfire in the distance.

I had nothing, and now I'll never have anything again,
so I dream a moment about this precious life.
There's no anger in my heart now, I don't think about revenge.
The world will be rebuilt again, let them ban my poems,
my voice will be heard at the foot of new walls.
Inside myself I live through everything that is still to come.
I don't look back. I know, not even memory, no magic
will save me—there's evil in the sky.
Friend, if you see me, shrug your shoulders and turn away.
Where the angel with the sword stood before,
now, is there anyone there.

April 30, 1944

In Hiding

I look at the mountain from the window,
it does not see me.
I hide, I write a poem,
not that it matters,
and I see the old grace. It is useless.
As before, the moon cuts into the sky
and the cherry opens.

   May 9, 1944

Picnic in May

The noise of the record player in the grass,
hoarse, breathless, hunted—
but there are no hunters here
only girls circling it
like burning flowers.

A little girl falls on her knees.
She changes the record.
Her back is brown, her legs white.
The music is bad
but her child's soul rises anyway.
It is gray, like clouds.

There are boys crouching. Awkward pretty words
stick to their lips like embers.
Their bodies swell with many little victories.
Calmly, when they have to,
they kill.

But they can still be men.
What is human about them is asleep
somewhere inside.
Say it, say that there is hope.

May 10, 1944

Landscape in a Dream

When the soot of the night drips,
when evening's fantasy withers in the sky,
in the deep-sea silence, the night
weaves bouquets of stars above me.

When the moon's head bleeds in the sky
and rings form where light hits the lake,
shadows cross the yellow land
and crawl up the edge of the hill.

And in the forest, flowing into a dance,
fish clap under the fearful nests,
under the swaying, dreamy eyes of leaves
they break the mirror surface.

Suddenly the landscape disappears,
on huge wings.
A bird, chased by terror,
is pushed across the clouded sky.

In my heart loneliness is sweeter
and death is a closer relative.

October 27, 1943–May 16, 1944

Fragment

I lived on this earth in an age
when man fell so low
he killed willingly, for pleasure, without orders.
Vile obsessions threaded his life,
he believed in false gods. Deluded, he foamed at the mouth.

I lived on this earth in an age
when it was an honor to betray and to murder,
the traitor and the thief were heroes—
those who were silent, unwilling to rejoice,
were hated as if they carried the plague.

I lived on this earth in an age
when if a man spoke out, he had to vanish
and could only chew his fists in shame—
drunk on blood and scum, the nation went lost its mind
and grinned at its savage fate.

I lived on this earth in an age
when a curse was the mother of a child,
when women were happy if they miscarried,
a glass of thick poison foamed on the table,
and the living envied the rotting silence of the dead.

I lived on this earth in an age
when the poets too were silent
and waited for Isaiah, the scholar
of words that scorched his lips, to speak again—
since only he could utter the right curse.

May 19, 1944

The Seventh Eclogue

Do you see night and the wild oakwood fence lined with barbed
        wire
and the barracks, so flimsy that the night swallows them?
Slowly the eye passes the limits of captivity
and only the mind, the mind knows how tight the wire is.
You see, dear, this is how we set our imaginations free.
Dream, the beautiful savior, dissolves our broken bodies
and the prison camp leaves for home.

Ragged, bald, snoring, the prisoners flee
from the black heights of Serbia to the lost lands of home.
Lands of home! Are there still homes there?
Maybe the bombs didn't hit, and they *are*, just like when we were
        "drafted"?
Next to me, on my right, a man whines, another one lies on my
        left. Will they go home?
Tell me, is there still a home where they understand all this?

Without commas, one line touching the other,
I write poems the way I live, in darkness,
blind, crossing the paper like a worm.
Flashlights, books—the guards took everything.
There's no mail, fog drifts over the barracks.

Frenchmen, Poles, loud Italians, heretic Serbs and dreamy
Jews live here in the mountains, among rumors.
One feverish body cut into pieces, still living one life,
it waits for good news, the sweet voices of women, a free, a
        human fate.
It waits for the end, a fall into infinite darkness, miracles.

I lie on the plank, like a trapped animal, among worms. The fleas
attack again and again, but the flies have quieted down.
Look. It's evening, captivity is one day shorter.
And so is life. The camp sleeps. The moon shines
over the land and in its light the wires are tighter.
Through the window you can see the shadows of the armed
          guards
thrown on the wall, walking among the noises of the night.

The camp sleeps. Do you see it? Dreams fly away.
Someone wakes up. He grunts, then turns in his tight space
and sleeps again. His face is white. I sit up awake.
The taste of a half-smoked cigarette in my mouth instead of the
          taste
of your kisses and the calmness of dreams.
I can't die, I can't live without you now.

Lager Heidenau, in the mountains above Zagubica
July, 1944

A Letter to My Wife

At the bottom of life, worlds without voices or sounds,
silence howls in my ears, I shout,
but no one answers from distant
Serbia knocked out by the war.
And you are far away. My dreams gather your voice—
I find it in my heart during the day—
so I'm silent, while many proud ferns,
cool to the touch, stand around me and hum.

I don't know when I'll see you again.
You who were certain, steady as a psalm,
beautiful as light, beautiful as shadow,
I could find you without a voice, without eyes.
Now you are in the landscape and appear
in front of my eyes from inside, where the mind sends out its
          images.
You were real, now you're a dream again.
Falling into the well of adolescence,

I question you, jealously. "Do you love me,
and one day, at the peak of my youth,
will you be my wife?" I hope again,
but, falling back on the road of daily life,
I know you are my friend, my wife—
and you are three wild borders away!
And autumn nears again. Will it forget me too and leave me here?
The memory of our kisses is so clear.

I believed in miracles but I forgot the days,
bomber squadrons fly over me.
I was just admiring your blue eyes in the sky,
but they disappeared and the bombs in the plane
wanted to fall. I live against them—
caged. I've thought about all
I hope for, I'll still find you.
I've walked all the miles of the soul for you—

and the roads of these countries. On deep red ashes,
in a rain of fire if I have to,
I'll use magic but I'll get back.
I'll be as tough as the bark on a tree,
the serenity of wild men who live in constant danger,
constant trouble, the calmness of weapons and power
will soothe me and, like a cold wave, the soberness
of the multiplication table will protect me.

Lager Heidenau, in the mountains above Zagubica
August–September, 1944

Root

Power glides in the root,
drinking rain, living in the earth,
and its fantasy is white snow.

It rises and breaks through the soil,
it crawls along secretly.
Its arm is like rope.

On the root's arm a worm sleeps
and a worm sticks to its leg.
The world is rotten with worms.

But the root goes on living below.
It is the branch, laden with leaves,
that it lives for, not the world.

This is what it feeds and loves,
sending exquisite tastes up to it,
sweet tastes out of the sky.

I am a root myself now,
living among worms.
This poem is written down there.

I was a flower. I became a root.
A lid of black earth locks me in.
The workers on my life are done.
A saw wails over my head.

> *Lager Heidenau, in the mountains above Zagubica*
> *August 8, 1944*

Like Memory

(À la Recherche)

Old, soft evenings, you too are better as memories!
Brightly lit table of poets and their young wives,
where do you slide in the mud of the past?
Where is the night when excited, happy friends
drank wine from fine-eyed, slim glasses?

Lines of poetry swam in the lamplight, bright-green
adjectives swayed on the frothy crest of verse,
the dead were alive, the prisoners at home, the missing,
dear friends, those who fell long ago, wrote poems.
The soil of Ukraine, Spain and Flanders lies on their hearts.

There were those who, unable to do anything against it,
gritted their teeth, ran into fire and fought.
And under the filthy night, while the company slept
uneasily around them, they thought about their rooms,
islands, caves for them in this society.

There were places they went to in sealed cattle cars,
they stood freezing and unarmed in the minefields.
There were places they went to willingly, weapons in hand;
silent, they went to fight in battles for a cause they believed in—
and now the angel of peace guards their dreams at night.

There were places... it doesn't matter. Where are the wise,
        wine-drinking days?
The quick summons reached them, pieces of poems,
wrinkles around the lips and under the eyes of young,
beautifully smiling women multiplied; in the silent years of the war
the girls who walked like angels grew fat.

Where's the night, the bar, the table under the linden trees?
And the living, where are the ones herded into battle?
In my heart I hear their voices, in my hand I grip their hands,
I quote their works, silhouettes of their bodies appear
and I measure them (silent prisoner) in the sorrowful Serbian
        heights.

Where's the night? That night will never come again.
Death changes the way we look at the past—
asleep in alien pastures and alien forests,
those who are not buried will sit at our table,
they will hide behind the smiles of the women and drink
        from our glasses.

Lager Heidenau, in the mountains above Zagubica
August 17, 1944

The Eighth Eclogue

Poet:

Greetings. You keep a good pace on this wild mountain road,
old man. Do wings lift you, does an enemy follow you?
Wings lift you, driven by passion, lightning explodes in your eyes.
Greetings, old man. Now I see you are one of the ancient
prophets, filled with rage, but which one are you, tell me?

Prophet:

I am Nahum, from the city of Elkosh.
I cried out against the sinful Assyrian city, Nineveh.
I cried the words of God. I was his sack full of anger!

Poet:

I know your ancient fury from your writings.

Prophet:

Yes, they lasted. But there is more sin now than ever,
and still, no one knows what God wants.
He has said that wide rivers will run dry,
that Carmel and Bashan will fall, that the flowers of Lebanon
will die. Mountains will shake. Everything will burn.
And all these things came to pass.

Poet:

Nations rushing to kill each other off,
man's soul is stripped bare, the way Nineveh was.
What's the use of speeches, what use are the swarms of savage,
ravenous, green locusts? Man is the most miserable of all animals!
Everywhere, infants are smashed against walls,
church steeples turn into torches, houses become ovens,
people burn inside. Factories drift away in smoke.
Filled with burning people, streets rumble and collapse.
The big beds of bombs burst into flame, huge clamps break open,
and like cowturds in a pasture, the shriveled bodies of the dead
are scattered in city parks. Everything happened
just as you said. Tell me, what made you come down here
from behind the ancient clouds?

Prophet:

Rage. Man is
again and again an orphan in the armies of pagans
who look like men—I would like to see the evil fortresses
fall again and I want to be a witness for the ages still to come.

Poet:

You have been a witness. And long ago, the Lord said through you:
"Let the fortresses filled with the spoils of war, the ones in which
there are bastions made out of dead bodies, beware!" But tell me,
has rage stayed alive in you this way for thousands of years,
stubborn, supernatural rage?

Prophet:

Long ago, the Lord touched my deformed mouth with a coal
the way he touched wise Isaiah's. With its embers
he questioned my heart. The live coal was red hot,
an angel held it with tongs. "Look, here I am, call me
to spread your words," I called after him.
And whomever the Lord sends once, he has no age,
and no rest. The angel's coal scorches his lips.
And tell me, what's a thousand years to the Lord? A butterfly's
          lifetime!

Poet:

How young you are, father, I envy you. How can I compare my
          little time
here to your frightening age? Like a pebble in a rushing
stream, even my time racing past wears me down.

Prophet:

You think. But I know your latest poems. Anger keeps you alive.
The anger of prophets and poets is related. It is food and drink for
the people! And if a man wants to, he can live on it, until
he reaches the land which that young disciple promised,
the rabbi who fulfilled the law and our words.
Come with me and teach that the hour is near, and
that country almost born. "Lord, what is your goal?"
I asked. "Behold, it is that land." Come, let us go. Let us gather
the people. Bring your wife and cut branches, make staffs.
A staff is good company for the wanderer. Look, give me that one.
There, that'll be mine. I like them better if they are gnarled.

> *Lager Heidenau, in the mountains above Zagubica*
> *August 23, 1944*

Forced March

You're crazy. You fall down,   stand up and walk again,
your ankles and your knees move
but you start again   as if you had wings.
The ditch calls you, but it's no use   you're afraid to stay,
and if someone asks why,   maybe you turn around and say
that a woman and a sane death   a better death wait for you.
But you're crazy.   For a long time
only the burned wind spins   above the houses at home,
Walls lie on their backs,   plum trees are broken
and the angry night   is thick with fear.
Oh, if I could believe   that everything valuable
is not only inside me now   that there's still home to go back to.
If only there were! And just as before   bees drone peacefully
on the cool veranda,   plum preserves turn cold
and over sleepy gardens   quietly, the end of summer bathes in
        the sun.
Among the leaves the fruit   swing naked
and in front of the rust-brown hedge   blond Fanny waits for me,
the morning writes   slow shadows—
All this could happen   The moon is so round today!
Don't walk past me, friend.   Yell, and I'll stand up again!

September 15, 1944

Postcard

1

From Bulgaria the huge wild pulse of artillery.
It beats on the mountain ridge, then hesitates and falls.
Men, animals, wagons and thoughts. They are swelling.
The road whinnies and rears up. The sky gallops.
You are permanent within me in this chaos.
Somewhere deep in my mind you shine forever, without
moving, silent, like the angel awed by death,
or like the insect burying itself
in the rotted heart of a tree.

In the mountains

Postcard

2

Nine miles from here
the haystacks and houses burn,
and on the edges of the meadow
there are quiet frightened peasants, smoking.
The little shepherd girl seems
to step into the lake, the water ripples.
The ruffled sheepfold
bends to the clouds and drinks.

> *Cservenka*
> *October 6, 1944*

Postcard

3

Bloody drool hangs on the mouths of the oxen.
The men all piss red.
The company stands around in stinking wild knots.
Death blows overhead, disgusting.

> *Mohács*
> *October 4, 1944*

Postcard

4

I fell next to him. His body rolled over.
It was tight as a violin string before it snaps.
Shot in the back of the head—"This is how
you'll end." "Just lie quietly," I said to myself.
Patience flowers into death now.
"Der springt noch auf," I heard above me.
Dark filthy blood was drying on my ear.

Szentkirályszabadja
October 31, 1944

About Miklós Radnóti

In 1946, when Miklós Radnóti's wife found his body, in the pockets of his trenchcoat was a notebook that contained all the poems the great Hungarian poet had written during his internment at a copper mine in Bor, Yugoslavia.

Radnóti was born a twin in Hungary in 1909. After receiving his diploma University of Szeged, he went to Budapest to teach, but despite his qualifications he was never appointed to the positions he deserved because he was a Jew. He spent some time in Paris (where he began writing the first poems for *Clouded Sky*), supported himself by translating and published many of his poems in major literary periodicals.

With other "progressive" intellectuals, Radnóti was at the center of opposition to the "conservative" regime of Regent Miklós Horthy, which allied itself with the Nazis in World War II. Beginning in 1940, he was sent to a number of forced labor camps. At one point he worked along the Ukrainian front, arming and disarming explosives; finally in 1944 he was taken to Bor, southeast of the Hungarian border. From there, the Fascists drove him and the rest of the prisoners across Hungary to the town of Abda, in the northwest of the country, where, no longer useful, the workers were beaten to death and thrown into a mass grave.

Surviving prisoners had smuggled copies of his poems out of the camp, but the five written in his last days, "Roots" and Postcards 1 through 4, were unknown until his wife discovered them in his grave.